Davidson 12/23/05 23.92

D0570736

Track Events

in Action

John Crossingham & Bobbie Kalman

Illustrations by Bonna Rouse

Crabtree Publishing Company

www.crabtreebooks.com

Created by Bobbie Kalman

Dedicated by Jeff Gogo
To Cody, the fastest kid in the 7th Grade

Editor-in-Chief
Bobbie Kalman

Writing team
John Crossingham
Bobbie Kalman

Substantive editor
Kelley MacAulay

Project editor
Kristina Lundblad

Editors
Molly Aloian
Kathryn Smithyman

Art director
Robert MacGregor

Design
Katherine Kantor

Cover design
Margaret Amy Reiach

Production coordinator
Katherine Kantor

Photo research
Crystal Foxton

Consultant
Pat Mooney, Head Cross-Country and Track and Field Coach,
Clarion University of Pennsylvania

Special thanks to
Josh Fenton, Kyle Emery, Eric Emery, Michael Emery,
and Cambridge Track and Field Club

Photographs
Marc Crabtree: pages 8, 12, 17 (all except top)
Icon SMI: Neil Tingle/Action Plus: page 14; Frank
    Faugere/DPPI: pages 24, 25, 28
© PHOTOSPORT.COM: pages 9, 13, 15, 18, 19, 20, 21, 22,
    23, 26, 31 (top)
DuaneHart/sportingimages.com.au: page 29
Other images by Corbis, Corel, Digital Stock, Image 100,
and Photodisc

Illustrations
All illustrations by Bonna Rouse

Crabtree Publishing Company

www.crabtreebooks.com   1-800-387-7650

Cataloging-in-Publication Data
Crossingham, John.
  Track events in action / John Crossingham & Bobbie Kalman;
illustrations by Bonna Rouse.
      p. cm. -- (Sports in action)
  Includes index.
  ISBN 0-7787-0339-8 (RLB) -- ISBN 0-7787-0359-2 (pbk.)
  1. Track and field--Juvenile literature. I. Kalman, Bobbie.
II. Rouse, Bonna, ill. III. Title.
  GV1060.55.C76 2004
  796.42--dc22
                                                    2004014181
                                                         LC

**Published in
the United States**

PMB16A
350 Fifth Ave.
Suite 3308
New York, NY
10118

**Published
in Canada**

616 Welland Ave.,
St. Catharines, Ontario
Canada
L2M 5V6

**Published in the
United Kingdom**

73 Lime Walk
Headington
Oxford
OX3 7AD
United Kingdom

**Published
in Australia**

386 Mt. Alexander Rd.,
Ascot Vale (Melbourne)
VIC 3032

Contents

What are track events?

Track events are foot races that test a runner's speed. Runners compete in races over different distances. Races are often held along with jumping and throwing events called **field events**. When these competitions are combined, they are known as **track-and-field meets**.

A popular sport

Track events are popular all over the world. Every four years, the world's best track athletes compete against one another in track events at the Olympic Games. Many children learn about and compete in track events at school. Track events are held at elementary schools, high schools, and universities. Some cities also have track clubs for people who enjoy competing in track events.

It takes years of practice for athletes to become skilled track athletes.

Ancient history

The first Olympic Games were held about 3,000 years ago in Olympia, Greece. Only men were allowed to participate in and watch the events. The Games included only one running race. Over the years, more track events were added. About 1,000 years later, the Olympic Games were stopped by a Roman emperor.

Back for good

In 1896, the Olympics started up again in Athens, Greece, with a focus on track-and-field events. These games were still for men only. Women were not allowed to compete in the Olympics until 1928. Today, the world's most important track-and-field competition is the Olympic Games.

Go the distance

Listed below are the main track events and their distances. All races are measured in meters (m). One meter measures a little more than one yard. Men and women run in separate races. Young athletes often run shorter distances than do experienced athletes.

Sprints: 50m (indoor), 100m, 200m, 400m

Hurdles: 100m, 110m, 300m, 400m

Relays: 4x100m, 4x400m, 4x800m

Mid-distance: 800m, 1500m, 1600m, 2000m

Steeplechase: 2000m, 3000m

Long distance: 3000m, 5000m, 10 000m

Marathon: 42.2km (26.2 miles)

Walks: 20km (12.4 miles), 50km (31 miles)

Keep reading to learn more about these track events!

The essentials

Track events are held on a course called a **track**. The track is also called the **oval** because it is oval in shape—it has two long sides, with wide, rounded turns. Each athlete runs in a separate **lane**. Lanes are between two-and-a-half and four feet (0.8-1.2 m) wide. Most tracks have eight lanes, which means that up to eight runners can race at once.

The surface of the track can be made of different materials, including dirt and pavement. Most tracks have **artificial surfaces**. Circling the track one time is called a **lap**. A single lap around the inside lane of the track is exactly 400 meters. Athletes must run additional laps for races that are longer than 400m. The track has lines to mark the start and finish lines of all races.

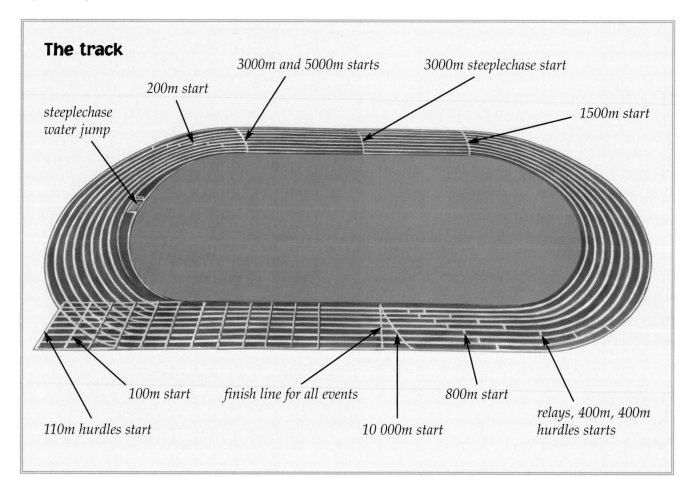

The track

3000m and 5000m starts

3000m steeplechase start

200m start

1500m start

steeplechase water jump

100m start   finish line for all events   800m start

110m hurdles start

10 000m start

relays, 400m, 400m hurdles starts

Get dressed

Choosing the right clothing can help you run faster! Track clothing is tight-fitting, but it is comfortable enough that you can move easily in it. The most common uniform for a track athlete is a pair of shorts and a sleeveless shirt called a **singlet**. Some runners wear one-piece uniforms. Boys and girls wear slightly different uniforms. During competitions, runners are identified by numbers that are pinned to their singlets.

Sweet feet

An athlete's shoes are his or her most important pieces of equipment. Runners use lightweight shoes that **mold**, or fit tightly around, the foot. Most track shoes have tiny spikes on the soles, near the fronts of the shoes. The spikes grip the track. A firm grip is important when an athlete runs around turns. Runners use shoes with spikes only on the track, however. They wear heavier shoes without spikes for training off the track.

A track uniform for a boy usually consists of a singlet and shorts. The runner can choose the length of his shorts. Some girls wear shorts that are similar to swimsuit bottoms, whereas others wear regular shorts.

spike

Training safely

You should never **train**, or practice, for track events on your own. You will become a better athlete with the help of a coach. You may already have a gym teacher or a coach at your school.

Listening to your coach's advice will help you learn new techniques, improve your skills, and correct any bad habits that may be slowing you down.

Your coach may encourage you to practice with other track athletes who are at the same skill level.

Listen to your body

People who run too hard or too often can injure their legs, feet, or ankles. Many people ignore the pain of these or other minor injuries. Even small injuries, however, can turn into major problems if they aren't checked by a doctor and allowed time to heal. If you are hurt, tell your coach. He or she may ask you to take a break from practice for a few days. Your coach may also tell you to use ice, bandages, or muscle creams to help heal any minor injuries.

Lean and mean

As an athlete, you must pay close attention to the foods that you eat. Ask your coach or doctor about which foods you should be eating for your level of activity. Remember, sprinters have different needs than do long-distance runners, so mention your event when talking to your doctor. Always drink plenty of water, even on the days when you're not practicing.

If you are running and start getting a cramp, slow down and walk for several minutes, then take a short rest.

Warming up

Running or walking can be very hard on your joints and muscles. It is important for you to stretch your muscles before and after each practice or competition. Begin by walking briskly for five or ten minutes to get your heart pumping and to warm up your muscles. Then perform the stretches shown on these pages. Stretching your muscles reduces the possibility of injuring yourself. Warm up in a sweatsuit to help keep your muscles warm while you are waiting to race.

Quadriceps stretch

Stand on your left foot. Bend your right leg behind you and grab your ankle with your right hand. Keep your knees close together. Pull gently on your right ankle until you feel a stretch in the front of your right thigh. Hold the stretch for a count of ten and then switch legs.

Ankle rotations

Sit with your right leg **extended**, or straight out in front of you. Bend your left leg until your lower leg is resting across your right thigh. Grab your left foot and gently move it in circles. When you have done ten circles, do ten more in the other direction. Remember to change legs!

Hip flexor stretch

Stand with your feet shoulder-width apart. Step out as far as you can with your right leg. Lower your left knee to the floor and place the top of your foot on the floor. Move your hips forward until your right knee is directly over your toes. Place your hands on your right thigh for support. Hold for fifteen seconds and then switch legs.

Hamstring stretch

Sit on the floor with your right leg straight in front of you. Bend your left leg and place your foot facing the inside of your right knee. Bend forward slightly until you feel a stretch up the back of your right leg. Hold for fifteen seconds. Repeat with your left leg extended.

Neck stretches

Stand with your legs shoulder-width apart and your arms by your sides. Slowly turn your head and look over your left shoulder, keeping the rest of your body still. Hold the stretch for ten seconds. Return your head to the starting position and then slowly turn your head to the right. Hold the stretch on that side. Return to the starting position. Slowly lower your head and look at your chest. Hold the stretch for ten seconds. Then gently tilt your head until you are looking up at the ceiling and hold that stretch.

Staying strong

To be a great track athlete, you will need to do more than just warm up and start running! Athletes spend time off the track performing exercises that strengthen their muscles. Stronger muscles mean more speed and **endurance**. Endurance is the ability to keep your body moving for a long time.

Push-ups and **crunches** are two great exercises for improving the strength of your muscles. Push-ups improve the strength of your upper body, including your chest, stomach, and shoulder muscles. Crunches strengthen your stomach muscles.

To perform a push-up, lie on the ground, facing down. Place your hands on the floor beneath your shoulders. Straighten your arms to push your body up. Your body should be in a straight line from your head to your toes. Your weight should be resting on your hands and your toes. Lower yourself down until your nose is about four inches (10 cm) from the floor. Repeat ten times.

To perform a crunch, lie on your back and put your hands behind your head. Bend your knees and place your feet flat on the ground. Press your lower back against the floor and slowly lift your shoulders off the floor. Lower yourself back down. Repeat ten times.

A balancing act

Athletes must have good balance to run around turns at high speeds. Good balance also improves your **posture**, or body position, while you run. To improve your balance, stand on one leg and close your eyes. Try holding this position for at least twenty seconds. Repeat this exercise on your other leg. To make the exercise more challenging, place your hands on your hips. This exercise also strengthens your ankles.

Get moving!

Sprinting, or running at top speed over short distances, is a great way to train for many types of races. Sprint for 20 to 30 meters and then walk around for a minute. Soon you'll be ready to do another fast run. Repeat this combination three or four times. These runs may last for only a few seconds, but they are very good for your leg muscles. Running up and down flights of stairs or jumping rope are other great exercises for sprinters.

Starting track practice with a 30m sprint gets your heart pumping without tiring you out for the rest of the practice.

Cooling down

When you finish a competition or track practice, it is important to cool down. Cooling down for ten to fifteen minutes allows your body temperature and breathing to return gradually to normal. The best way to cool down is to walk around the track after you run. After you have cooled down, do some stretches to prevent your muscles from becoming stiff and sore.

Sprints

The fastest track races are called **sprints**. The most common sprints are the 100m, 200m, and 400m. Indoor track-and-field meets also have 50m races. Sprinters must stay in their own lanes for the entire race. The key to good sprinting is having strong muscles.

Sprinters must be able to run at top speed for the entire race. The arm and leg muscles of professional sprinters are stronger than the muscles of other runners. Having strong muscles gives runners the explosive power they need to win.

*Each runner's **finish** is timed. A finish is the exact second when a runner's chest crosses the finish line. The first runner across the finish line wins the race. Most sprinters lean forward at the finish line to improve their time.*

Arms and legs

While sprinting, pump your arms as you push forward with your legs. Pumping your arms can help you gain speed and thrust your body forward. Having good posture also helps you run faster, but try not to lean too far forward while running. Instead, **run tall**, or keep your back straight and hold up your head.

The different races

Each sprint is slightly different. The length of one side of a track is 100m, so the 50m and 100m races are run in straight lines. In the 200m and 400m races, however, the runners must go around the turns of the track. Running the turns is a skill sprinters must master. The 400m is an especially difficult sprint—athletes must run at top speed for longer distances, including around two turns.

While running around a turn, lean your body slightly into the turn. Do not lean too far, or you will lose your balance.

A good start

Nothing is more important to a sprinter than starting a race well. It is difficult to win a race, especially the 100m, after a slow start. Sprinters practice their starts over and over. They use **starting blocks**. Starting blocks are small raised platforms from which runners push off to help them get the most explosive starts.

The **starting gun**, shown on page 17, is a piece of equipment that signals the beginning of the race and starts a timer that times the runners. If a runner starts before he or she hears the sound of the starting gun, that runner has made a **false start**. Crossing the starting line too soon may cause a runner to be **disqualified**, or forced to leave the race.

Straight or staggered?

Races of different lengths have different starting points on the track. During 200m and 400m races, runners must round the turns of the track. One lap around a track's inside lane is a shorter distance than one lap around its outside lane, however. To make sure all the runners travel the same distance, longer races begin with **staggered starts**. In a staggered start, the starting blocks of the athletes are placed at different spots along the track. The finish line is still a straight line, however. The 50m and 100m races do not have staggered starts. These races are short enough to be run in straight lines.

Three positions

Sprints begin with a **three-stage count**. The traditional way of performing the three-stage count is by saying, "On your mark, get set, go!" The starting gun is fired at the same moment as the word "Go!" is said. Each of the three steps that start a race requires a different body position. The body positions are shown below.

1. "On your mark!"

Kneel down and place your feet in the starting block. Put all your weight on the **balls** *of your feet. Put your hands behind the starting line, shoulder-width apart.*

2. "Get set!"

Raise your eyes slightly and lift your hips above your shoulders. Keep your back straight. Your weight is now on your hands, and your feet are firmly against the block.

3. "Go!"

Push away strongly from the block. Build up speed by pumping your arms and keeping your body low for the first few meters.

Hurdles

Hurdles races are similar to sprints, but there are some important differences. During hurdles races, athletes must **clear**, or leap over, small fences called hurdles as they run. Athletes must carefully time their sprints, or they will knock over the hurdles. The most common hurdles races are women's 100m races, men's 110m races, and 300m and 400m races, in which both men and women compete. The height of the hurdles depends on the distance of the race and the sex of the athletes. In races for beginners, lower hurdles and shorter distances are used than in races for experienced athletes.

Hurdles are designed to fall forward if they are bumped. You are allowed to knock over a hurdle during a race, but doing so will slow you down.

Follow the leader

While clearing a hurdle, your **lead leg** is the first leg that you lift up and over the hurdle. Your other leg is called the **trail leg**. You will likely use the same lead leg for short-distance races, but for longer races, you will need to **alternate**, or switch, your lead leg.

Not too high

During a race, your goal should be to leap only as high as needed to clear the hurdle. High jumps will get you over the hurdles, but these jumps will also slow you down and waste your energy. If you are having problems timing your jumps, lower the hurdles and concentrate on clearing them without slowing down. Once your jumps are smooth, slowly raise the hurdles back up to improve your hurdling.

trail leg

lead leg

1. As you take off, lift the knee of your lead leg and then extend the leg. Lean forward with your upper body. Reach forward with the arm that is opposite to your lead leg to help you balance. As you go over the hurdle, pull up the knee of your trail leg, keeping both your knee and toe pointing outward so they don't hit the hurdle. Your head and shoulders should face forward.

2. Prepare to land on your lead leg as soon as you cross over the hurdle. You should land on the ball of your foot and continue sprinting toward the next hurdle.

Teamwork

Relay races or relays are the only track events in which teams of people compete against one another. Each relay team has four people, each of whom run a **leg**, or section, of the race. The races are named for the distances the runners travel. The most common relays are the 4x100m, 4x400m, and 4x800m. The "x" in the event name is pronounced "by." In a 4x100m relay, each of the four team members runs a 100m leg of the race.

Pass it off

Running one at a time, the team members carry a **baton** from the start of the race to the end. As one team member nears the end of his or her leg of the race, he or she passes the baton to the next runner. The **handoff** occurs in a 20m section of the track called the **exchange zone**. The handoff must occur successfully in this area before the next runner can move on. In the 4x100m race, the runner receiving the baton can begin running 10m before the start of the exchange zone. The team's two best runners usually run the first and last legs.

*A **medley** is a type of relay race in which each athlete runs a different distance during his or her leg. Common medleys are 100m, 200m, 300m, and 400m.*

In the zone

The runner arriving in the exchange zone with the baton is called the **incoming runner**. The runner waiting to receive the baton is called the **outgoing runner**. The best way to pass the baton is by placing it down into the outgoing runner's upturned palm. Try passing the baton to the hand of your teammate that is opposite to your hand. For example, if the baton is in your left hand, pass it into your teammate's right hand. Before each race, discuss with your teammates and coach which hands you will use.

1. Wait for your teammate at the start of the exchange zone. Just before your teammate arrives, begin running. Get ready to reach back and grab the baton.

2. Your teammate will pass the baton to you as you both enter the exchange zone. If you are racing in the 4x100m race, don't look back or it will cost you valuable time! As soon as you feel the baton, grab it firmly and sprint out of the exchange zone.

Mid-distance races

Mid-distance races are 800m, 1500m, and sometimes 2000m long. These distances are much too long for athletes to sprint the entire time! Athletes usually sprint for only the last 200m of mid-distance races. Instead of speed, the runners rely on endurance and on **strategies**, or plans, to gain advantages over their **opponents**.

Out-standing starts

Athletes competing in races that are 800m or longer do not begin the races with starting blocks or staggered starts. Instead, they begin the races with **standing starts**, or with all the runners standing behind a starting line. The runners must stay in their lanes until they reach the first turn of the track. When athletes are past the first turn, they are allowed to cross into one another's lanes. They compete to gain the inside lane because it is the shortest distance around the track.

During a standing start, place one foot ahead of the other. Stand on the balls of your feet so you will be ready to spring forward when you hear the starting gun.

Keep it simple

The best way to win a mid-distance race is to save some of your energy for the end of the race. Sprint from the starting line to gain a quick lead, but then slow your pace a bit to save energy. Breathe normally and concentrate on having good posture throughout the entire race. You will have a better chance to win if you stay close behind the leader—you only need to run as fast as he or she runs. As the finish line nears, find the right moment to sprint forward and take the lead.

Long-lasting power

It's not easy to sprint at the end of a race! Mid-distance runners train hard to increase their endurance. They do this by running long distances in practice. For example, runners training for the 800m race run 1500m in practice. When they run the 800m, they have the extra power they need to sprint to the finish line.

Whenever possible, train with other runners. They will push you to sprint to the finish line, instead of jogging for the entire practice.

Steeplechase

The steeplechase is a challenging race that combines running with leaping over **barriers**, or steel fences, and **water jumps**. Most steeplechase races are between 2000m and 3000m long. Steeplechase barriers stand 36 inches (0.9 m) high for men and 30 inches (0.8 m) high for women.

Unlike hurdles, the barriers can't be knocked over. In fact, if runners get tired, they sometimes climb over the barriers! Steeplechase water jumps are shallow pools that are about ten feet (3 m) long. A water jump is located right after every fourth barrier.

Up and over

A steeplechase barrier that is followed by a water jump requires a different kind of leap. To make it over the water jump, you'll need to step onto the top of the barrier and then push off it and continue running. To do this, extend your lead leg toward the barrier. Place the ball of your foot on its edge. Next, tuck your trail leg behind you. Finally, push off the barrier with your lead leg. Before landing, extend your arms out in front of you. Although you are allowed to land in the water during a race, you should try to jump over the entire pool as often as possible.

Getting physical

Advanced steeplechase runners usually compete in 3000m races. The 3000m event is about two miles of leaping, running, and splashing through water. Unlike hurdles, the barriers in steeplechase reach across the entire width of the track. Runners have no choice but to go over them! Runners do not need to stay in their own lanes, so there is often physical contact between them as they struggle for the best positions.

Going the distance

Long-distance races are 3000m, 5000m, and even 10 000m long! The longest race—which measures about 42km (26 miles) long—is a **marathon**. Young athletes rarely compete in long-distance races. They usually don't start running the 3000m race until they are about fourteen years old.

Slow and steady

A long-distance race requires more endurance than almost any other sports event in the world! Even the best 10 000m runners need a half hour to complete the race! Unlike sprinters, good long-distance runners save their energy during most of the race by keeping their bodies relaxed. For example, long-distance runners hold their arms loosely at their sides, as opposed to pumping their arms quickly.

Tricky, tricky

Distance runners often run in tight groups called **packs**, shown above. The best runners are able to control the pack by changing their speed slightly throughout the race. For example, by speeding up a little, you can cause the group to panic and run harder. Remember, your opponents are trying to play the same tricks on you, so stay focused!

Tour the great outdoors

The marathon is a track event, but most of it takes place off the track! At the Olympics, marathons begin and end on the track, but most of the race takes place on city streets and country roads. Road surfaces are less even than are the surfaces of tracks. Marathon runners must remain alert in order to handle any unexpected bumps in the road. Running a marathon takes months of training. Most people never even attempt to run a marathon, so just finishing one is an amazing achievement!

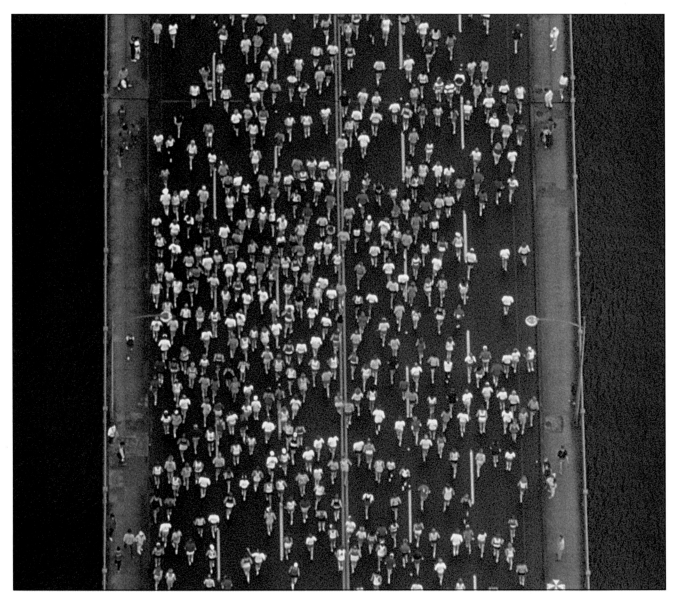

Marathons are held in big cities around the world. One of the most famous marathons is the Boston marathon.

Race walking

Race walking is the only track event in which running is not allowed. Instead, a race walker uses a special style of walking step to achieve high speeds without running. Race walkers must be very patient and determined. The longest race walking event is 50km (31 miles)—that's longer than a marathon! There is also a 20km (12 mile) walk. Younger athletes walk in 1500m and 3000m races.

Walk, don't run!

The rules in race walking are strict. One foot must always be in contact with the ground. A walker is not allowed to **lift**, or have both feet off the ground at once, as a runner does. A walker's front leg must be straight when it touches the ground. Judges carefully watch each athlete. If an athlete is caught lifting or does not have a straight front leg, he or she gets a warning. An athlete who gets three warnings is disqualified.

Walk the walk

Don't let the name fool you—walking is a difficult event. Many of the strategies used by race walkers are the same as those used by long-distance runners. Race walkers try to keep their motions smooth while racing, so they won't waste their energy. The walkers pump their arms strongly at their sides to help them move forward. They also move their hips from side to side to stretch their legs so that one foot is always on the ground. Practice walking on a straight line, so that each foot lands on the line, pointing straight ahead. Always keep your head up and your back straight as you walk. Start slowly. It is important to get the technique right, before you build up speed.

1. To race walk, step forward with your right foot by planting it into the ground, heel first. Shift your hips to the left to allow your right foot to extend as far forward as possible. Keep your left foot flat on the ground. Then push off with the toes of your left foot and place your right foot flat on the ground.

2. Bend your left leg and swing your left foot forward as you extend that leg. Continue to move forward by using the same technique described in Step One. As you walk, shift your hips from side to side so that one foot lands directly in front of the other. Pump your arms for extra power.

The more, the merrier

Several track-and-field events are **multi-event competitions**, or competitions in which a single athlete competes in several events. The **decathlon** is a ten-event competition for men. The **heptathlon** is a seven-event competition for women. Similar multi-event competitions are the **triathlon** and the **pentathlon**. The athletes in multi-event competitions may not be the world's best in any of the individual events, but they have the ability to do well in all the events combined. World-class multi-event athletes spend years training before they are ready to win competitions.

A perfect ten

The decathlon stretches over two days and includes the following track events: 100m, 400m, 1500m, and 110m hurdles. It also includes these field events: **long jump**, **shot put**, **high jump**, **javelin**, **pole vault**, and **discus**. Points are awarded to the **decathlete**, or decathlon athlete, based on his performance in each event. These points are then added up to determine the winner. Decathletes are well-balanced athletes who are flexible, strong, and quick.

The 1500m is the final event of the decathlon.

Heptathlon

The heptathlon is a two-day, seven-event competition. A heptathlon includes the following events: 200m, 800m, 100m hurdles, shot put, javelin, long jump, and high jump. **Heptathletes**, or heptathlon athletes, must be in excellent shape to master all seven events.

Pentathlon

The pentathlon is similar to the heptathlon, but it has only five events, and both men and women participate. Each pentathlon features different events, depending on the age of the athletes. A pentathlon usually includes a short hurdles race, a mid-distance race of 800m or 1500m, and three field events.

Three's a charm

The triathlon is different from other multi-event competitions because it includes two events that are not track-and-field events. **Triathletes**, or triathlon athletes, swim the first leg of the race, cycle the second leg, and then run the last leg of the race. Although distances of each leg vary from race to race, all triathlons are tests of endurance. The **ironman triathlon** ends with a full marathon!

Glossary

Note: Boldfaced words that are defined in the text may not appear in the glossary.

artificial surface A playing surface made of a substance, such as rubber, which is made by people

ball The rounded wide part of the sole of the foot between the toes and the arch

baton A hollow metal tube carried by relay racers

discus A field event in which an athlete throws a wooden or plastic disc as far as possible

handoff The act of handing a baton to a teammate in a relay race

high jump A field event in which an athlete jumps over a high horizontal bar

ironman triathlon A competition in which an athlete performs a 2.4 mile (3.9 km) swim, a 112 mile (180.2 km) bike ride, and a 26.2 mile (42.2 km) run

javelin A field event in which an athlete throws a metal spear

long jump A field event in which an athlete jumps as far as possible

opponent A person who competes against another person

pole vault A field event in which an athlete uses a long pole to clear a high horizontal bar

shot put A field event in which an athlete throws a heavy metal ball as far as possible

water jump A small area of water that immediately follows a barrier in the steeplechase event

Index

1 2 3 4 5 6 7 8 9 0   Printed in the U.S.A.   4 3 2 1 0 9 8 7 6 5